The
Wild Canary

by Richard Rensberry

illustrated by

Linda Faith Widing

This book is dedicated to
all the organic farmers
that work in harmony
with our natural world.

The wild canary is forever
grateful.

The Wild Canary

He tweets his song
sunflower bright,

sporting feathers
of gold
and wings like night.

He bathes in glory
from a thistle's crown,

his lady finch
flitting 'round
      and 'round.

It's a courtship dance
that he joins with

                    mirth,

twittering aloft
then back to earth.

Sweet love unfolds
atop an apple tree,

a blossoming Dutch
with a nest for three.

From eggs petite,
speckled and blue,

the chicks come
　　　　　helpless
and featherless, too.

They nurse and grow
among tasseling oats

to lift man's spirit
with musical notes.

They feast and flock
through Autumn's hold,

then follow their
                    instinct
to escape the cold.

Fleeter and stronger than a northern

squall,

all gold finch migrate
come first snowfall.

The End

Glossary:

aloft- in the air

courtship- romantic reaches

Dutch- an early sour apple

fleeter- more agile, athletic

glory- great beauty

gold finch- wild canary

instinct- inner compass, natural knowing

migrate- fly south for the winter

mirth- merriment and joy

petite- delicate and small

squall- a strong storm

tasseling- going to seed

thistle- a prickly plant with a purple flower

In the woods of Lewiston, Michigan
I found my passion of drawing
wildlife in rapid sketch style.

I add another dimension to my
sketches by creating a unique
background for each animal.

By manipulating the light, shadow,
props, and photography, I
capture an illusion of their
environment, and bring the
animals to life!

The process has become a
trademark of my animal
sketches.

Linda Faith Widing

The Wild Canary

He tweets his song
sunflower bright,
sporting feathers of gold
and wings like night.

He bathes in glory
from a thistle's crown,
his lady finch
flitting 'round and 'round.

It's a courtship dance
that he joins with mirth,
twittering aloft
then back to earth.

Sweet love unfolds
atop an apple tree,
a blossoming Dutch
with a nest for three.

From eggs petite,
speckled and blue,
the chicks come helpless
and featherless, too.

They nurse and grow
among tasseling oats
to lift man's spirit
with musical notes.

They feast and flock
through Autumn's hold,
then follow their instinct
to escape the cold.

Fleeter and stronger
than a Northern squall,
all gold finch migrate
come first snowfall.

Richard Rensberry 6/13/25

Be sure to check out

Kirtland's Warblers

another magical children's book

by author Richard Rensberry

and illustrator Linda Faith Widing

KIRTLAND'S

WARBLERS

RICHARD
RENSBERRY

Illustrated by
Linda Faith Widing

Blessings from all our feathered friends!

www.ingramcontent.com/pod-product-compliance
Lightning Source LLC
Chambersburg PA
CBHW041229270326
41935CB00006B/61